Kansuko

A New Game Based on Classic Sudoku

4880 Lower Valley Road • Atglen, PA 19310

Printed in the United States of America

Jonathan Meck

Designed by Danielle D. Farmer
Type set in Helvetica Neue LT Pro

ISBN: 978-0-7643-4203-5
Printed in The United States of America

Published by Schiffer Publishing, Ltd.
4880 Lower Valley Road
Atglen, PA 19310
Phone: (610) 593-1777; Fax: (610) 593-2002
E-mail: Info@schifferbooks.com

For the largest selection of fine reference books on this and related subjects, please visit our website at **www.schifferbooks.com**. You may also write for a free catalog.

This book may be purchased from the publisher.
Please try your bookstore first.

We are always looking for people to write books on new and related subjects. If you have an idea for a book, please contact us at proposals@schifferbooks.com

Schiffer Books are available at special discounts for bulk purchases for sales promotions or premiums. Special editions, including personalized covers, corporate imprints, and excerpts can be created in large quantities for special needs. For more information contact the publisher.

In Europe, Schiffer books are distributed by
Bushwood Books
6 Marksbury Ave.
Kew Gardens
Surrey TW9 4JF England
Phone: 44 (0) 20 8392 8585; Fax: 44 (0) 20 8392 9876
E-mail: info@bushwoodbooks.co.uk
Website: www.bushwoodbooks.co.uk

Contents

Introduction

About Kansuko

Kansuko is a fun variation of the popular Sudoku number game made up of three 3 x 3 grids and an additional sum column. Each grid contains every number from 1 through 9. No number will be repeated inside of a 3 x 3 grid. Each of the four columns, including the sum column, also contain the numbers 1 through 9, with no repeats. Take the last digit from the sum of the numbers in each row to arrive at the numbers in the sum column. For instance, 6 + 3 + 7 = 16, so the number 6 would appear in the sum column. The same number may appear in a row in both the grid and the sum column.

Solving Kansuko

Many of the same techniques used to solve a Sudoku puzzle can also be used to solve Kansuko. In the example on the opposite page, the second box of the first column can be determined from looking at the other grids. The number 7 already appears in the second and third grids in the second and third columns. Since a number can only appear in a grid or column once, 7 must appear in the first column of the first grid.

With a number already in the third box, the 7 must go in either the first or second box of the first column. If the 7 were placed in the first box, the sum of that row (7 + 2 + 5) would be 14, so a 4 would need to go in the sum column. There is already a 4 in the sum column, so therefore, the only place that the 7 can go is in the second box in the first column.

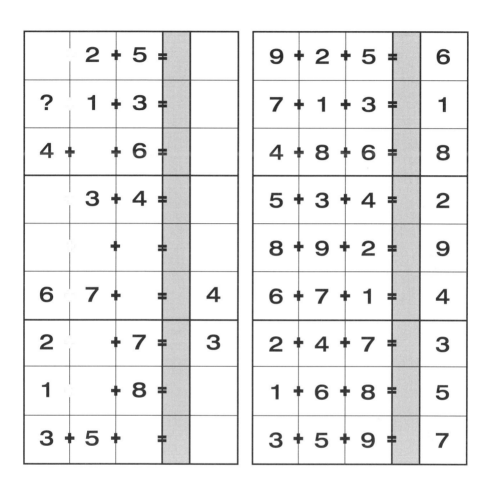

	2 + 5 =			9 + 2 + 5 =	6
?	1 + 3 =			7 + 1 + 3 =	1
4 +	+ 6 =			4 + 8 + 6 =	8
	3 + 4 =			5 + 3 + 4 =	2
	+ =			8 + 9 + 2 =	9
6 7 +	=	4		6 + 7 + 1 =	4
2	+ 7 =	3		2 + 4 + 7 =	3
1	+ 8 =			1 + 6 + 8 =	5
3 + 5 +	=			3 + 5 + 9 =	7

Continue to use this type of logic and reasoning to help solve even the toughest of puzzles. In some instances, it may be helpful or necessary to write down potential numbers that may work in a box. As you fill in more numbers in the puzzle, erase or cross out numbers that can no longer fit. When only one number is left, that's the number that belongs there!

Remember, you should never have to guess to complete a puzzle!

For more Kansuko puzzles and solutions, visit www.kansuko.com.

Beginner
Puzzles

Puzzle #1

4 +	+ 2 =		5
+ 8 +	=		
1 + 7 +	=		
+	+ 4 =		
9 + 6 +	=		3
2 +	+ =		4
6 +	+ =		7
+	+ 1 =		2
7 + 4 +	=		

Start Time: _____   End Time: _____

11

Puzzle #2

	+		+		=		
	+	9	+	4	=		8
	+		+	1	=		4
8	+		+		=		
1	+		+	3	=		
6	+		+	8	=		1
	+	2	+	9	=		
	+	1	+		=		7
3	+		+		=		
	+		+	6	=		6

Solution on page 130

Start Time: _____   End Time: _____

+	+ 2	=		5
1 +	7 +	=		
+	5 + 6	=		9
+	+	=		8
4 +	9 +	=		
6 +	2 +	=		3
+	+	=		6
5 +	+ 9	=		
7 +	+ 4	=		

Start Time: _____   End Time: _____

Solution on page 130

8 +		+ 6	=	
	+ 1	+	=	2
3 +	4	+	=	4
5 +		+ 1	=	
	+	+	=	3
6 +	8	+	=	
	+	+ 9	=	6
7 +	6	+	=	
1 +		+	=	8

Start Time: _____   End Time: _____

Solution on page 130

5 +		+ 6 =		
+ 2	+	=		3
+ 9	+	=		8
9 +		+ 4 =		
+ 1	+	=		9
7 +		+ 3 =		
+ 4	+	=		2
+ 6	+	=		6
2 +		+ 8 =		

Solution on page 130

Start Time: _____   End Time: _____

15

Puzzle #6

6 +	+	=		7
9 +	+ 5	=		
+ 1	+ 3	=		
4 + 8	+	=		
+	+ 6	=		5
3 + 5	+	=		
+ 9	+	=		8
+ 3	+ 4	=		
5 +	+	=		3

Solution on page 130

Start Time: _____   End Time: _____

	+		+		=		8
	+		+	1	=		4
	+	5	+		=		3
	+		+	2	=		6
	+	4	+	7	=		
	+		+	5	=		7
3	+		+	9	=		
6	+		+		=		1
	+	2	+	8	=		

Start Time: _____   End Time: _____

17

Puzzle #8

9 +	+ 5 =			
+	+ 2 =			1
7 +	+ =			9
+ 7 + 8 =				
+ 2 + =				2
+ 3 + =				7
2 +	+ =			8
+ 5 + 3 =				
8 + 4 + =				

Start Time: _____   End Time: _____

Solution on page 130

1 +	2 +		=	
+	+	6	=	3
+	3 +	4	=	
6 +	+	7	=	
2 +	+	9	=	
5 +	1 +		=	
3 +	6 +		=	
+	+	1	=	2
+	+		=	6

Start Time: _____   End Time: _____

Puzzle #10

	+ 4 +	9 =		
	+ 3 +	=		5
2 +	+ 1	=		
	+	8 =		3
5 +	+ 6	=		
9 +	+	=		4
4 + 5 +	=			
1 + 9 +	=			
6 +	+ 2 =			

Start Time: _____   End Time: _____

Solution on page 130

20

	+	3	+	5	=		
6	+		+	8	=		
	+	2	+		=		7
5	+		+		=		2
	+		+	3	=		9
1	+		+	7	=		
9	+	5	+		=		
	+		+	4	=		8
8	+		+	6	=		

Start Time: _____   End Time: _____

4 +	+	=		7
6 +	+	=		6
5 +	8 +	=		
+	9 +	3 =		
+	+	6 =		8
2 +	+	=		4
+	7 +	1 =		
9 +	+	4 =		
8 +	2 +	=		

Start Time: _____   End Time: _____

Solution on page 130

Puzzle #13

	+	3	+		=	
8	+		+		=	7
	+		+	7	=	
	+		+	8	=	2
	+	1	+	6	=	
	+	4	+	2	=	9
9	+		+	1	=	
4	+	7	+		=	
	+	2	+	3	=	

Start Time: _____   End Time: _____

Puzzle #14

	+	9	+		=		
2	+		+	4	=		
	+		+	8	=		
4	+	7	+		=		2
3	+	6	+		=		
	+	8	+		=		9
6	+	2	+		=		
5	+		+	7	=		
8	+	4	+		=		

Solution on page 131

Start Time: _____   End Time: _____

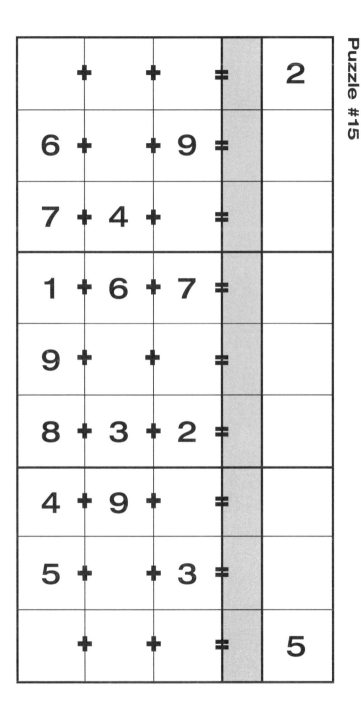

				2
6 +		+ 9 =		
7 +	4 +	=		
1 +	6 +	7 =		
9 +		+ =		
8 +	3 +	2 =		
4 +	9 +	=		
5 +		+ 3 =		
+		+ =		5

Start Time: _____   End Time: _____

Puzzle #16

			=	
	+ 4	+ 6	=	8
9	+ 2	+	=	
	+ 1	+ 7	=	
5	+	+ 9	=	
7	+	+	=	4
	+ 3	+	=	9
	+ 5	+ 8	=	
	+ 7	+	=	5
	+	+	=	3

Solution on page 131

Start Time: _____   End Time: _____

7 +	+ 9 =			
+	+ 5 =		5	
2 +	+ 3 =			
9 +	+ 4 =		6	
+	+ =		1	
5 +	+ 6 =			
+ 4	+ 2 =			
+	+ =		9	
+	+ 1 =		2	

Start Time: _____   End Time: _____

Puzzle #18

5	+	+	=	4
	+ 4	+ 2	=	
6	+	+	=	2
1	+	+	=	3
	+	+ 6	=	7
4	+	+ 8	=	
7	+	+	=	1
2	+	+ 9	=	
	+ 6	+ 4	=	

Start Time: _____   End Time: _____

Solution on page 131

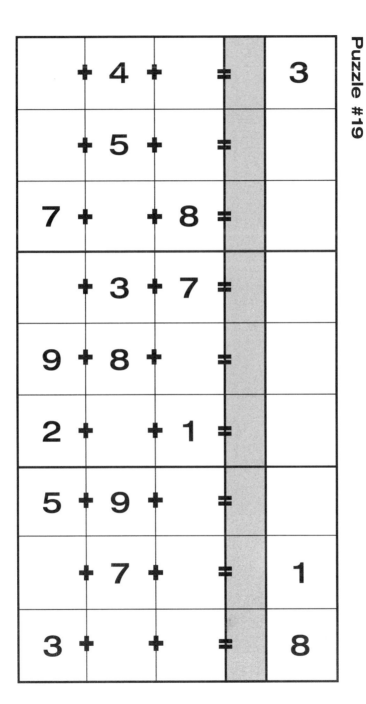

+ 4 +		=		3
+ 5 +		=		
7 +	+ 8	=		
+ 3 + 7		=		
9 + 8 +		=		
2 +	+ 1	=		
5 + 9 +		=		
+ 7 +		=		1
3 +	+	=		8

Solution on page 131

Start Time: _____   End Time: _____

5 +		+ 7 =		
+	1 +	=		3
2 +	4 +	=		
7 +	+	=		
+	9 +	2 =		2
8 +	3 +	=		
3 +	+	1 =		
6 +	+	=		9
+	+	=		5

Start Time: _____ End Time: _____

Solution on page 131

Solution on page 131

9 +		+ 7	=	
+	8	+	=	6
5 +		+ 3	=	
7 +	3	+	=	4
+		+ 9	=	3
+		+	=	8
+		+ 5	=	5
+	9	+	=	
1 +		+	=	9

Start Time: _____   End Time: _____

Puzzle #22

	+	1	+		=	1
	+	3	+	5	=	
	+		+	7	=	
3	+		+	8	=	
	+		+		=	3
	+	2	+	4	=	
6	+	4	+	9	=	
	+	8	+		=	2
7	+		+	2	=	

Solution on page 131

Start Time: _____   End Time: _____

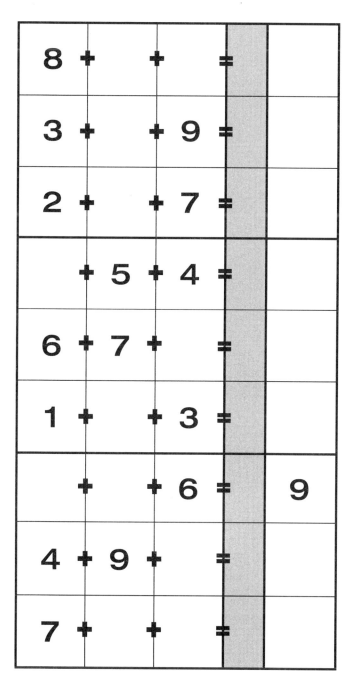

8 +	+	=		
3 +	+ 9	=		
2 +	+ 7	=		
+ 5	+ 4	=		
6 + 7	+	=		
1 +	+ 3	=		
+	+ 6	=		9
4 + 9	+	=		
7 +	+	=		

Start Time: _____   End Time: _____

33

Puzzle #24

7 +	+	=		4
+ 6	+ 5	=		
+ 3	+ 1	=		
8 +	+	=		6
+ 2	+	=		7
+ 5	+	=		2
1 + 7	+	=		
9 +	+ 2	=		
+	+	=		5

Solution on page 131

Start Time: _____   End Time: _____

34

+	3	+ 5	=	7
+		+ 1	=	
+		+ 6	=	2
+	6	+	=	9
+		+ 2	=	5
+	1	+ 7	=	
6 +		+ 3	=	8
7 +	2	+	=	
+		+	=	4

Start Time: _____   End Time: _____

+ 3	+ 7	=		
4 +	9 +	=		
+ 2	+ 1	=		
2 +	+	=		9
8 +	+	=		2
+ 7	+ 6	=		
7 +	+ 2	=		7
9 +	+	=		5
+ 6	+	=		

Start Time: _____   End Time: _____

+ 1	+ 4	=		
8 + 7	+	=		
+	+	=		6
5 +	+	=		
+ 2	+ 7	=		
9 +	+ 1	=		
+ 5	+ 6	=		
+ 8	+ 2	=		7
+	+	=		3

Start Time: _____   End Time: _____

Puzzle #28

			=	
4 +	6 +		=	1
+	+		=	
9 +	8 +		=	
+	2 +		=	4
6 +	5 +		=	
+	3 +		=	3
2 +	9 +		=	
5 +	+		=	2
7 +	+		=	

Solution on page 132

Start Time: _____   End Time: _____

+	3	+	7	=	
+		+	5	=	1
+	9	+		=	
+		+		=	
8	+		+		=	9
3	+		+	4	=	
+	7	+		=	
+		+		=	3
4	+	1	+		=	7

Start Time: _____   End Time: _____

Puzzle #30

1 +	4 +		=	
8 +		+ 2	=	
	+	+ 9	=	
7 +		+ 5	=	
2 +		+	=	3
	+	+	=	4
	+	+ 1	=	7
	+ 9	+ 7	=	
	+ 8	+	=	6

Start Time: _____   End Time: _____

Intermediate
Puzzles

	+ 7 +	=	8
1 +	+	=	3
+ 3 + 6	=	
+ 6 +	=	
+ 2 +	=	6
7 + 4 +	=	2
6 +	+	=	
3 +	+	=	
+ 9 + 8	=	1

Start Time: _____   End Time: _____

Puzzle #32

8 +	+	=		4
5 + 3 +		=		2
+	+	=		9
7 + 1 +		=		
2 +	+ 9	=		6
4 +	+	=		
+ 4 + 2		=		
3 +	+ 6	=		
1 +	+	=		3

Start Time: _____   End Time: _____

Solution on page 132

	+		+		=	
8	+		+	5	=	
	+	1	+	7	=	
9	+		+		=	1
	+		+	1	=	
5	+		+		=	
	+		+	9	=	
	+	2	+	8	=	7
4	+		+	3	=	

Solution on page 132

Start Time: _____   End Time: _____

Puzzle #34

	+		+		=		
	+		+	3	=		2
6	+		+	2	=		
	+		+	9	=		4
	+	9	+	4	=		5
1	+		+		=		3
	+	6	+		=		7
	+		+	1	=		8
8	+	7	+		=		
9	+		+		=		6

Solution on page 132

Start Time: _____   End Time: _____

5	+ 8	+	=	9
	+	+ 4	=	
	+	+	=	
3	+	+	=	6
4	+ 5	+	=	
	+ 6	+ 8	=	
1	+ 9	+	=	
6	+	+	=	5
	+ 7	+	=	7

Solution on page 132

Start Time: _____   End Time: _____

Puzzle #36

+ 1 +		=		5
+ 4 + 6 =				
+ 8 +		=		3
9 +	+ 3 =			
+ 6 +		=		2
+ 5 + 1 =				
+ 2 +		=		
+ 3 +		=		6
1 +	+	=		8

Solution on page 132

Start Time: _____   End Time: _____

	+ 3 + 7 =	
	+ + 4 =	
5 + 1 + =		
3 + 6 + =		
	+ 8 + 9 =	
	+ 7 + =	6
8 + + =		
7 + 5 + =		5
	+ 4 + =	

Start Time: _____   End Time: _____

Puzzle #38

+	+	=		4
1 +	4 +	=		
+	9 +	8 =		
7 +	+	4 =		
8 +	+	=		2
9 +	+	=		7
2 +	8 +	=		
4 +	+	5 =		
3 +	+	7 =		

Solution on page 133

Start Time: _____   End Time: _____

Puzzle #39

	+		+	5	=		2
7	+		+	8	=		
	+		+	2	=		4
5	+		+		=		5
8	+		+	3	=		
	+	7	+		=		
3	+		+		=		8
2	+	5	+		=		
1	+		+		=		1

Start Time: _____   End Time: _____

Puzzle #40

	+		+		=		
	+	6	+	1	=		
	+	4	+		=		
3	+		+	8	=		
	+		+	7	=		
	+	9	+	2	=		7
8	+	1	+		=		
7	+	8	+		=		
	+	2	+	6	=		
	+	5	+		=		9

Solution on page 133

Start Time: _____   End Time: _____

___ +	6 +	9 =		
3 +	___ +	7 =		
2 +	5 +	___ =		
___ +	___ +	2 =		
1 +	8 +	___ =		
___ +	4 +	3 =		
9 +	___ +	1 =		2
5 +	___ +	4 =		
___ +	3 +	___ =		7

Solution on page 133

Start Time: _____   End Time: _____

Puzzle #42

5 +	+ 3	=		
+ 1	+	=		2
+ 6	+ 4	=		
+ 9	+	=		1
+ 7	+	=		5
+ 2	+	=		9
+ 3	+ 1	=		
+	+	=		4
6 +	5 +	=		

Solution on page 133

Start Time: _____   End Time: _____

8 +	5 +		=	
1 +	9 +		=	
+	+	2	=	2
3 +	7 +		=	
+	+		=	4
+	+	6	=	3
7 +	+		=	5
2 +	+	9	=	
4 +	+		=	1

Solution on page 133

Start Time: _____   End Time: _____

Puzzle #44

	+	5	+	4	=	
	+		+	9	=	8
3	+		+		=	
5	+		+		=	2
2	+	9	+		=	
	+		+		=	9
8	+	2	+		=	
6	+	4	+		=	7
	+		+	1	=	

Solution on page 133

Start Time: _____   End Time: _____

	+		+	1	=
	+		+	5	=
	+	2	+	8	=	3
6	+	5	+		=
8	+		+	7	=
	+		+	9	=	2
1	+		+	4	=
7	+		+		=	1
5	+		+		=	6

Solution on page 133

Start Time: _____   End Time: _____

Puzzle #46

6 +		+ 5 =		
4 +	3 +	=		
+		+ 7 =		
3 +		+ 6 =		
9 +		+ 4 =		
+	2 +	=		
+		+ =		3
+		+ 9 =		
+	5 +	3 =		

Solution on page 133

Start Time: _____   End Time: _____

	+	2	+		=		1
	+	4	+		=		
7	+		+		=		
	+		+		=		6
4	+		+	8	=		
	+	6	+		=		
	+		+	6	=		
	+	8	+	4	=		3
	+	7	+	9	=		

Solution on page 133

Start Time: _____   End Time: _____

Puzzle #48

	+		+	=	
	+	2	+	=	1
5	+		+	=	8
	+		+	3 =	
	+		+	=	
	+	1	+	=	7
	+		+	5 =	9
	+	6	+	2 =	2
8	+		+	9 =	

Start Time: _____   End Time: _____

Solution on page 133

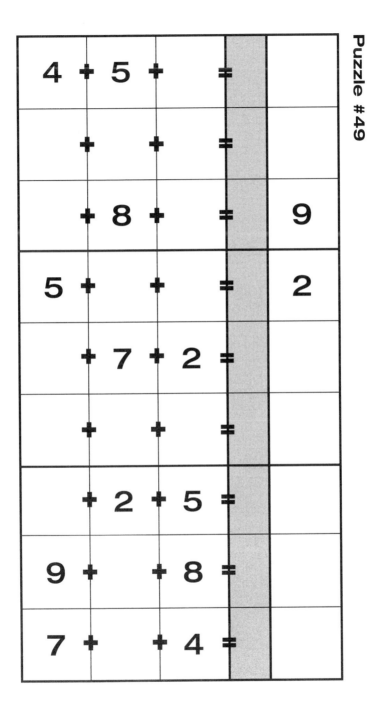

4 +	5 +	+	=	
+	+	=		
+	8 +	+	=	9
5 +	+	=		2
+	7 +	2 =		
+	+	=		
+	2 +	5 =		
9 +	+	8 =		
7 +	+	4 =		

Start Time: _____   End Time: _____

Puzzle #50

2 +	6 +		=	7
+		1	=	3
+		+	=	5
6 +		+ 8	=	
+		+	=	2
3 +		+ 4	=	
8 +	2 +		=	
1 +	4 +		=	
+		+ 7	=	

Solution on page 134

Start Time: _____   End Time: _____

+		+	=	**8**
+	**9**	+	=	
8 +	**4**	+	=	
+		+ **9**	=	
+	**5**	+ **7**	=	
+		+ **6**	=	
+	**6**	+	=	**7**
5 +		+	=	**6**
7 +	**1**	+	=	

Start Time: _____   End Time: _____

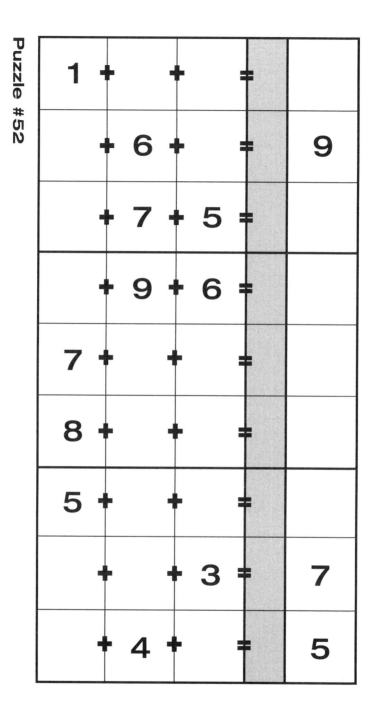

Puzzle #52

1	+	+	=	
	+ 6 +		=	9
	+ 7 + 5		=	
	+ 9 + 6		=	
7	+	+	=	
8	+	+	=	
5	+	+	=	
	+	+ 3	=	7
	+ 4 +		=	5

Solution on page 134

Start Time: _____   End Time: _____

	+		+ 9	=	
	+		+ 3	=	2
	+ 8	+		=	6
6	+		+	=	
	+		+	=	9
1	+		+	=	1
	+ 6	+ 4		=	
	+		+ 1	=	
9	+		+ 2	=	

Start Time: _____   End Time: _____

Puzzle #54

2 +	+	=		9
+	+	=		
8 + 4 +	=			
7 +	+ 3 =			
+	+	=		4
+	+ 5 =			
+ 7 + 1 =				
9 +	+	=		
+ 6 + 8 =				

Start Time: _____   End Time: _____

Solution on page 134

	+	+	=	8
7	+ 6	+	=	
9	+	+	=	1
	+	+	=	
3	+	+ 9	=	
	+ 2	+ 8	=	
	+ 7	+	=	
8	+ 9	+ 5	=	
	+	+	=	

Solution on page 134

Start Time: _____   End Time: _____

Puzzle #56

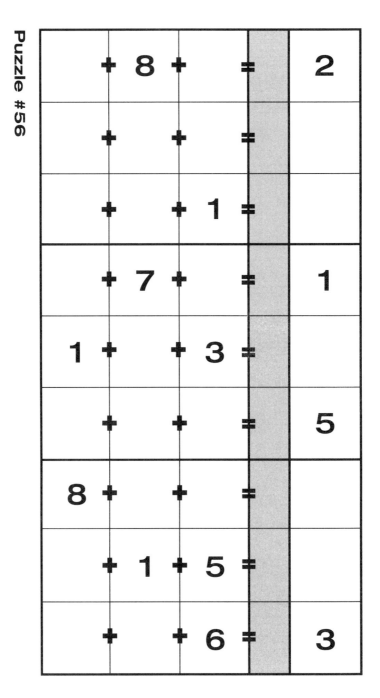

	+	8	+		=		2
+			+		=		
+			+	1	=		
+		7	+		=		1
1	+		+	3	=		
+			+		=		5
8	+		+		=		
+		1	+	5	=		
+			+	6	=		3

Start Time: _____   End Time: _____

Solution on page 134

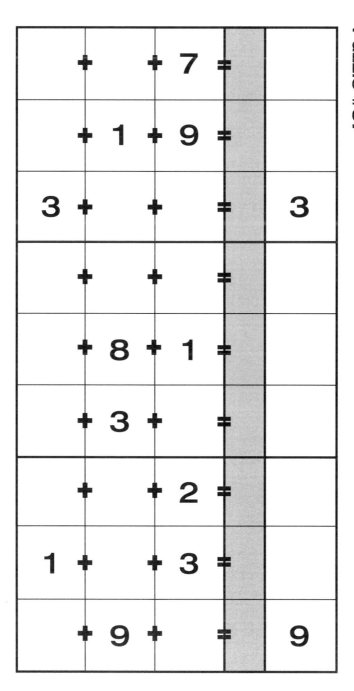

Solution on page 134

Start Time: _____   End Time: _____

Puzzle #58

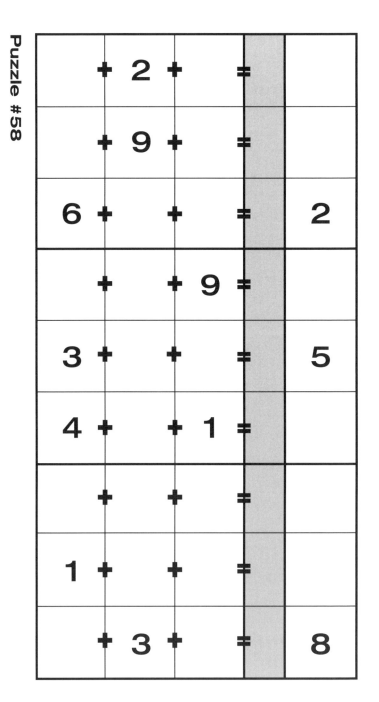

	+	2	+		=		
	+	9	+		=		
6	+		+		=		2
	+		+	9	=		
3	+		+		=		5
4	+		+	1	=		
	+		+		=		
1	+		+		=		
	+	3	+		=		8

Solution on page 134

Start Time: _____   End Time: _____

	+	7	+		=	1
	+	9	+		=	5
	+		+		=	
2	+		+		=	4
6	+		+	8	=	
	+	3	+		=	
4	+		+		=	
	+		+		=	6
	+		+		=	7

Solution on page 134

Start Time: _____   End Time: _____

Puzzle #60

	+	7	+		=	
6	+		+		=	
5	+	9	+	3	=	
2	+		+		=	
	+	1	+		=	6
	+		+	9	=	
8	+		+		=	
	+	5	+	6	=	
	+		+		=	9

Solution on page 134

Start Time: _____   End Time: _____

Expert
Puzzles

6 +	1 +		=	4
2 +		+	=	
+		5	=	8
+	9 +	3	=	
7 +		1	=	
4 +		2	=	
+		+	=	5
+	7 +		=	
+	2 +	6	=	

Start Time: _____   End Time: _____

Puzzle #62

	+	+	=	3
	+ 9	+ 5	=	
	+ 2	+ 7	=	
3 +		+ 8	=	
	+ 5	+ 4	=	
	+	+	=	
	+	+	=	
7 +		+ 9	=	4
5 +	4 +		=	

Solution on page 135

Start Time: _____   End Time: _____

Solution on page 135

		+		+		=	
1	+		+		=		3
	+	2	+	8	=		
3	+	4	+		=		
	+		+	6	=		1
	+	5	+		=		5
	+	9	+	7	=		
	+		+		=		
	+	1	+		=		6

Start Time: _____   End Time: _____

Puzzle #64

7 +	+	=		2
+	+	=		
+	9 +	=		4
+	7 +	3 =		
2 +	+	1 =		7
+	+	=		
+	2 +	=		8
+	6 +	=		1
+	3 +	9 =		

Start Time: _____   End Time: _____

Solution on page 135

Solution on page 135

	+		+		=	
2	+		+		=	9
	+	3	+	8	=	
1	+		+	4	=	
	+	7	+		=	
	+		+	5	=	
	+	5	+		=	8
	+		+	2	=	4
9	+		+		=	3

Start Time: _____   End Time: _____

Puzzle #66

6 +	+	+	=	
+	+ 2	=		8
+ 3	+	=		6
+	+ 6	=		9
+	+	=		
2 + 9	+	=		
+ 2	+ 3	=		
7 +	+	=		
+ 6	+	=		5

Start Time: _____   End Time: _____

Solution on page 135

	+	4	+	1	=		
	+		+		=		6
	+		+	3	=		
3	+		+		=		8
	+	7	+	4	=		
1	+		+	5	=		
	+		+		=		
	+	3	+		=		9
	+	1	+	2	=		

Solution on page 135

Start Time: _____   End Time: _____

Puzzle #68

	+		+		=	
4	+		+	7	=	
8	+	3	+		=	
	+		+		=	
2	+		+		=	1
	+	4	+	3	=	
5	+		+		=	
3	+		+		=	9
	+		+	6	=	4

Start Time: _____   End Time: _____

Solution on page 135

Solution on page 135

7 +	5 +		=	
+		+	=	7
+	3 +	8	=	
+		+	=	9
5 +		+ 7	=	
+		+ 1	=	
+		+	=	
3 +	1 +		=	
6 +		+ 5	=	

Start Time: _____   End Time: _____

83

Puzzle #70

7 +	+	=		
9 +	+	=		
+	+ 8	=		7
+ 5	+	=		6
+ 6	+	=		
+ 1	+ 9	=		
2 +	+	=		4
1 + 7	+	=		
+	+	=		

Start Time: _____   End Time: _____

Solution on page 135

	+ 8	+ 1	=	
7	+ 4	+	=	6
	+	+	=	
	+ 1	+ 7	=	
	+	+	=	8
	+	+ 8	=	4
6	+	+	=	
	+	+	=	
	+ 7	+ 4	=	

Start Time: _____   End Time: _____

Puzzle #72

	+ 4	+ 2	=	
5 +		+	=	
6 +		+	=	4
	+	+	=	
2 +		+	=	8
	+	+ 7	=	1
	+ 5	+ 8	=	
	+	+	=	
7 +		+	=	

Start Time: _____   End Time: _____

Solution on page 135

	+		+		=		
8	+	5	+		=		
	+		+	4	=		
	+		+	5	=		2
	+	6	+	7	=		
	+	3	+	2	=		
	+		+		=		1
	+		+	9	=		
	+		+	6	=		

Solution on page 136

Start Time: _____   End Time: _____

Puzzle #74

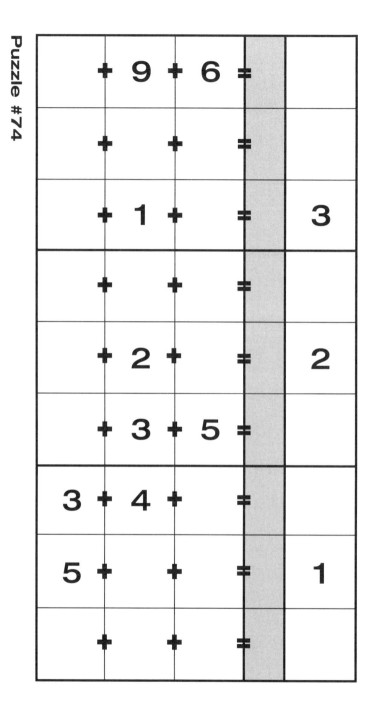

	+ 9 + 6 =	
	+ + =	
	+ 1 + =	3
	+ + =	
	+ 2 + =	2
	+ 3 + 5 =	
3 + 4 + =		
5 + + =		1
	+ + =	

Start Time: _____   End Time: _____

Solution on page 136

	+	8	+		=	1
	+		+		=	8
	+		+		=	6
	+	4	+	8	=	
	+	3	+	1	=	
	+		+		=	
	+		+	3	=	
9	+	6	+		=	
	+		+		=	

Solution on page 136

Start Time: _____   End Time: _____

Puzzle #76

	+		+		=		7
2	+		+		=		
	+	3	+		=		
	+		+	7	=		
	+	2	+		=		
	+	5	+	4	=		
	+		+		=		
	+	8	+	6	=		
	+	4	+		=		1

Start Time: _____   End Time: _____

Solution on page 136

3 +	2 +	+	=	
+	8 +	+	=	8
5 +	+	+	=	
6 +	+	2 +	=	
+	5 +	+	=	9
+	+	+	=	
+	4 +	+	=	
+	+	+	=	
+	+	+	=	6

Solution on page 136

Start Time: _____   End Time: _____

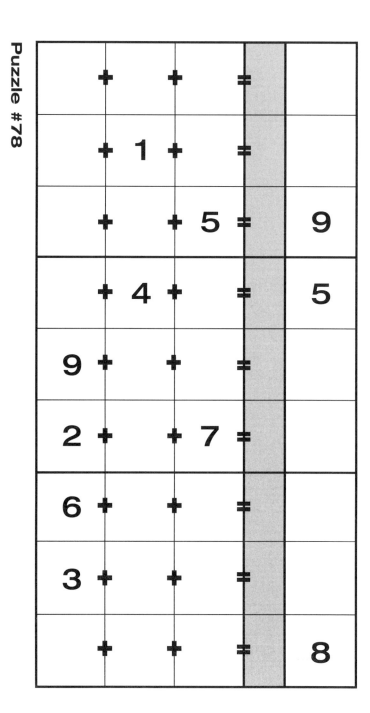

Start Time: _____   End Time: _____

Solution on page 136

6	+	+	=	4
	+	+	=	8
	+	+	=	
+	9	+ 8	=	
+		+ 4	=	1
+		+	=	
+	7	+	=	
4	+	+	=	
+	1	+	=	2

Start Time: _____   End Time: _____

Puzzle #80

	+ 5 +		=		
3 +	8 +		=		
	+	+	=		
9 +	+ 3		=		
	+	+	=		
	+ 2 +		=		8
	+ 6 + 5		=		
	+	+	=		4
1 +	+		=		

Start Time: _____   End Time: _____

Solution on page 136

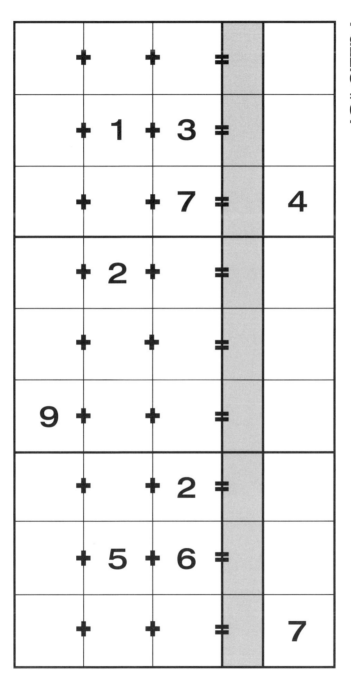

Start Time: _____   End Time: _____

Puzzle #82

	+		+	=
	+	+ 8	=	
	+ 2	+	=	8
	+	+ 5	=	
9 +		+	=	
	+	+	=	2
8 +		+	=	1
4 +		+	=	
	+ 1	+	=	

Start Time: _____   End Time: _____

Solution on page 136

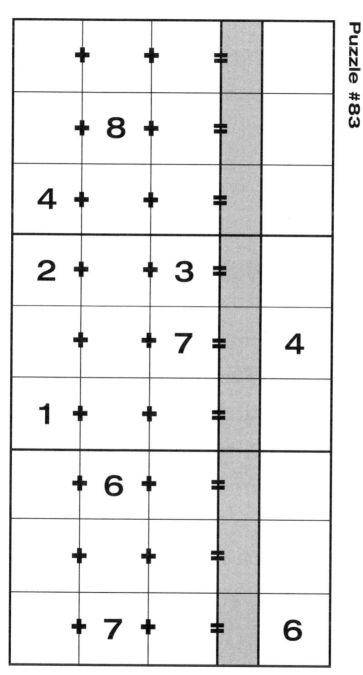

Start Time: _____   End Time: _____

Puzzle #84

			=		
2 +	6 +		=		
+	+		=		7
5 +	+		=		
1 +	3 +		=		
+	+		=		
+	+		=		4
+	+ 2		=		
+	+		=		
9 +	+ 7		=		

Start Time: _____   End Time: _____

Solution on page 136

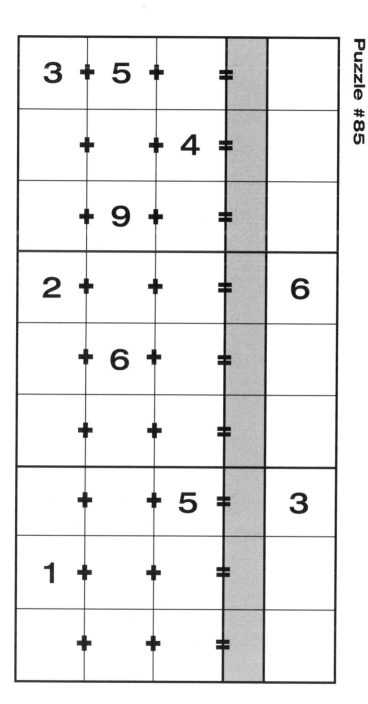

3 +	5 +		=	
+	+	4	=	
+	9 +		=	
2 +	+		=	6
+	6 +		=	
+	+		=	
+	+	5	=	3
1 +	+		=	
+	+		=	

Start Time: _____   End Time: _____

	+	7	+		=		7
	+	9	+		=		
	+		+		=		
	+		+		=		
	+	2	+		=		5
	+		+	4	=		
	+	1	+		=		4
	+		+		=		
5	+		+		=		3

Start Time: _____   End Time: _____

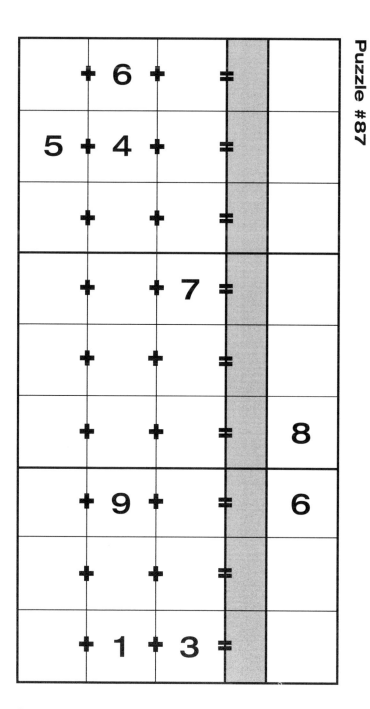

	+	6	+	=	
5	+	4	+	=	
	+		+	=	
	+		+	7	=	
	+		+	=	
	+		+	=	8
	+	9	+	=	6
	+		+	=	
	+	1	+	3	=	

Solution on page 137

Start Time: _____   End Time: _____

Puzzle #88

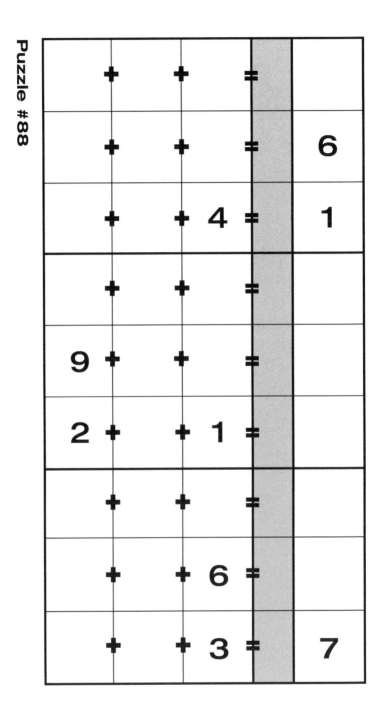

	+		+		=		
	+		+		=		**6**
	+		+	**4**	=		**1**
	+		+		=		
9	+		+		=		
2	+		+	**1**	=		
	+		+		=		
	+		+	**6**	=		
	+		+	**3**	=		**7**

Start Time: _____   End Time: _____

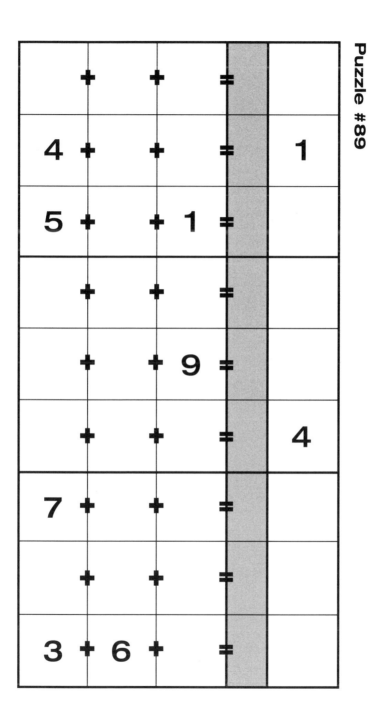

Solution on page 137

Start Time: _____   End Time: _____

Puzzle #90

1 +	+	=		1
+	5 +	+	=	
3 +	+	8 =		
+	+	=		
+	+	1 =		
6 +	+	=		
+	+	=		
+	+	4 =		
+	+	5 =		7

Solution on page 137

Start Time: _____   End Time: _____

Kansuko Varieties

Islands
No Fives
Hide & Seek
Krazy Kansuko

Islands

For this Kansuko variety, there are three "Islands"—one in each 3 x 3 grid. That means that each grid and column will only contain 8 numbers, though they still must be from 1 through 9. When adding a row to get the sum, the Islands are simply not included.

	+	+ 7	=	
4 +	+	=		3
8 +	+ 5	=		
+	+	=		4
6 +	+ 2	=		
+	+ 1	=		8
+	+ 3	=		6
2 +	+	=		1
5 +	+	=		

Start Time: _____   End Time: _____

	+	+	=	**6**
	+ **6** +	=		**3**
	+ **9** +	=		
	+	+	=	**9**
	+	+ **2** =		**5**
	+ **5** + **7** =			
8 +	+	=		
	+ **1** +	=		**4**
5 +	+ **9** =			

Start Time: _____   End Time: _____

Solution on page 137

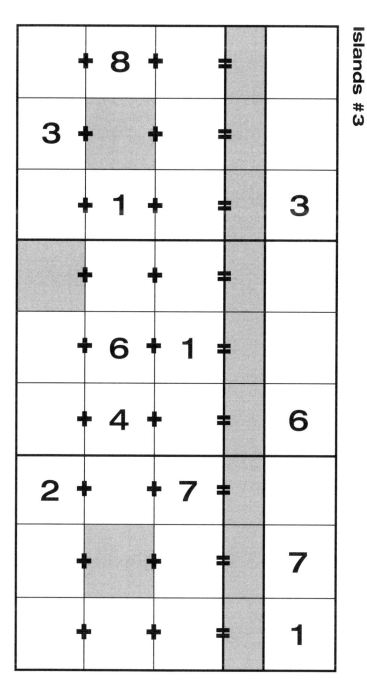

Start Time: _____   End Time: _____

Islands #4

	+		+ 5	=	9
	+ 9	+		=	
4	+	+		=	
3	+	+		=	7
2	+ 4	+		=	
	+	+		=	8
	+	+		=	
8	+ 2	+		=	
5	+	+		=	5

Solution on page 137

Start Time: _____   End Time: _____

No Fives

This Kansuko variety shakes up the players. Instead of using the numbers 1 through 9, you now must use the numbers 0, 1, 2, 3, 4, 6, 7, 8, 9. Essentially, all 5s have been replaced with 0s. That means you will have a zero in each grid and column, including the sum column!

No Fives #1

+ 4 +	=		**1**
+ + 1	=		**6**
+ 6 + 7	=		
6 + +	=		**0**
+ 2 +	=		**8**
4 + 8 +	=		
3 + +	=		**7**
1 + +	=		**4**
+ 9 + 2	=		

Solution on page 137

Start Time: _____   End Time: _____

9 +	+	3 =		
+	6 +	+	=	8
7 +	4 +	+	=	
+	+	8 =		
+	2 +	+	=	3
+	+	6 =		
2 +	+	+	=	
+	+	0 =		7
+	+	4 =		9

Solution on page 137

Start Time: _____   End Time: _____

No Fives #3

	+		+	=	**1**
	+	**4**	+	=	
9	+		+	**8** =	
2	+		+	=	**8**
	+	**8**	+	=	
	+		+	**1** =	
	+		+	=	**4**
7	+		+	=	**7**
3	+		+	**6** =	

Solution on page 138

Start Time: _____   End Time: _____

+	+ 8	=		
+	+ 6	=		
2 +	9 +	=		
+	+	=		6
+ 1	+ 3	=		
+	+	=		4
+ 7	+	=		
4 +	+	=		
+ 6	+	=		1

Solution on page 138

Start Time: _____   End Time: _____

Hide & Seek

For this puzzle, you'll have to seek out your starting numbers! The clues below link you back to a specific box on a previous puzzle. Find the number in that box, and fill it in at the designated spot in this puzzle! The bolded clues are the minimum necessary to complete the puzzle, but you can fill in as many as needed. You can look up previously completed puzzles or use the completed puzzles in the back of the book.

Hide & Seek #1

Puzzle #	Old Location	New Location
#1	A5	B4
#4	B6	D8
#54	B9	C4
#20	D2	A8
#7	C6	D3
#31	A6	A2
#33	D4	A5
#12	B7	B9
#58	D9	C2
#41	C8	A9
#71	D5	A7
#80	B1	B3
#49	A1	D7
#25	D4	A3
#76	B5	B1
#13	C7	D1
#5	D8	D5
#22	A4	B6
#47	B1	D6
#59	D8	B8

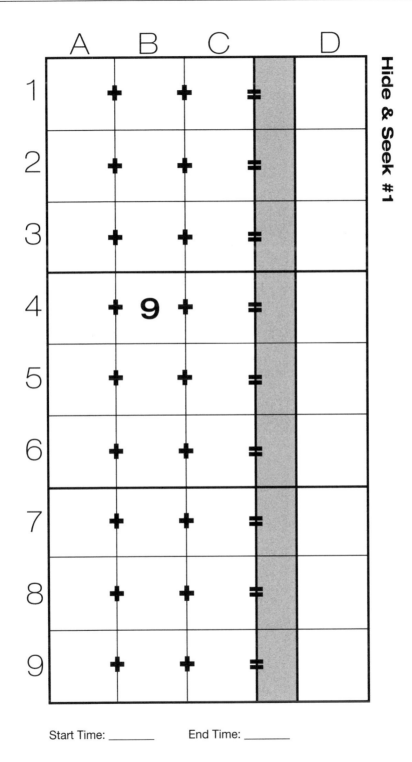

Solution on page 138

Start Time: _____   End Time: _____

Hide & Seek #2

Puzzle #	Old Location	New Location
#1	A1	C7
#68	D5	C3
#23	A1	A8
#18	D5	B4
#26	D4	C5
#2	A8	D2
#44	D4	D7
#37	A2	A1
#79	B7	C1
#19	A6	C6
#41	B3	C8
#50	D3	D6
#46	B6	A9
#21	B2	D1
#86	B6	B6
#5	B5	A4
#62	D8	A5
#70	A7	B2
#65	A9	B9
#28	A1	D3

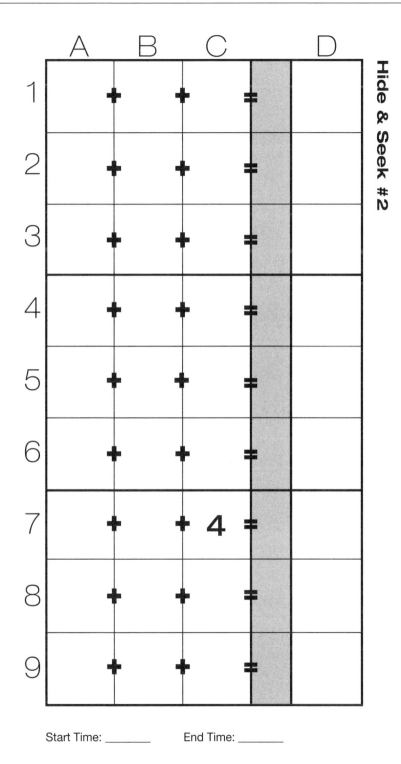

Start Time: _____   End Time: _____

Solution on page 138

Hide & Seek #3

Puzzle #	Old Location	New Location
#1	D5	B5
#29	B8	A4
#38	A9	C9
#25	B6	D4
#40	A2	A1
#51	C3	A9
#8	C3	C5
#77	D8	B3
#21	D4	B1
#33	A6	A8
#14	A6	C7
#35	D5	C2
#90	A7	A6
#74	D4	D8
#58	A7	D3
#66	A4	B6
#80	C9	B8
#45	B7	D2
#49	B6	D7

Solution on page 138

Start Time: _____   End Time: _____

Hide & Seek #4

Puzzle #	Old Location	New Location
#36	A9	D2
#14	C1	B5
#38	B6	D8
#22	D7	A9
#50	D6	D5
#18	A9	A7
#63	B7	D1
#22	C8	B3
#82	D1	C8
#89	C1	C4
#3	A7	B9
#75	B8	A1
#52	D3	B8
#20	C2	D6
#51	C7	A4
#62	C1	D7
#28	B3	C3
#76	B4	A6
#39	A2	A2

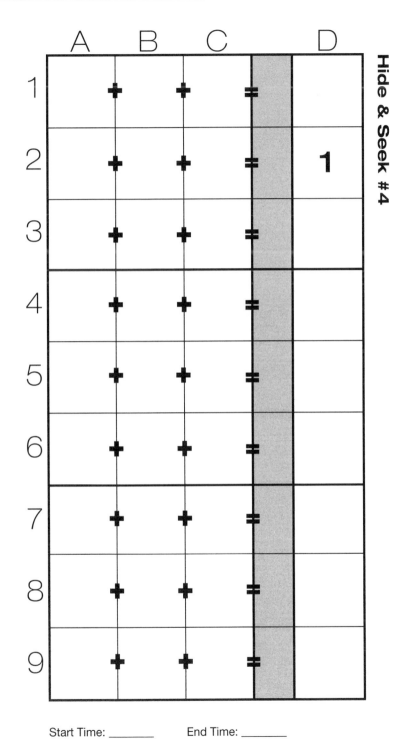

Solution on page 138

Start Time: _____ End Time: _____

Krazy Kansuko

It's just like a normal Kansuko, quadrupled! Four separate puzzles are joined together to make one giant puzzle, interlocking at each corner. Take your time and work your way through this Krazy puzzle!

Krazy Kansuko #1

	9			6	2		3	8	
1	1		5	4		9		7	9
5	8		4		7		2		2
6	2			8	1	4			3
2		6						1	
	5	4					4	9	
8	7					3		8	
	4		2	7	1				6
				3		8		2	
		1	9		2	7		4	
	3	4		6	7				

Start Time: _____   End Time: _____

Krazy Kansuko #2

Start Time: _____   End Time: _____

Solution on page 140

Solutions

Puzzle #1

4 + 9 + 2 = 5
5 + 8 + 6 = 9
1 + 7 + 3 = 1
3 + 1 + 4 = 8
9 + 6 + 8 = 3
2 + 5 + 7 = 4
6 + 2 + 9 = 7
8 + 3 + 1 = 2
7 + 4 + 5 = 6

Puzzle #2

5 + 9 + 4 = 8
7 + 6 + 1 = 4
8 + 3 + 2 = 3
1 + 5 + 3 = 9
6 + 7 + 8 = 1
4 + 2 + 9 = 5
9 + 1 + 7 = 7
3 + 4 + 5 = 2
2 + 8 + 6 = 6

Puzzle #3

9 + 4 + 2 = 5
1 + 7 + 3 = 1
8 + 5 + 6 = 9
3 + 8 + 7 = 8
4 + 9 + 1 = 4
6 + 2 + 5 = 3
2 + 6 + 8 = 6
5 + 3 + 9 = 7
7 + 1 + 4 = 2

Puzzle #4

8 + 5 + 6 =
9 + 1 + 2 =
3 + 4 + 7 =
5 + 9 + 1 =
2 + 7 + 4 =
6 + 8 + 3 =
4 + 3 + 9 =
7 + 6 + 8 =
1 + 2 + 5 =

Puzzle #5

5 + 3 + 6 = 4
4 + 2 + 7 = 3
8 + 9 + 1 = 8
9 + 8 + 4 = 1
6 + 1 + 2 = 9
7 + 5 + 3 = 5
3 + 4 + 5 = 2
1 + 6 + 9 = 6
2 + 7 + 8 = 7

Puzzle #6

6 + 4 + 7 = 7
9 + 2 + 5 = 6
8 + 1 + 3 = 2
4 + 8 + 9 = 1
2 + 7 + 6 = 5
3 + 5 + 1 = 9
1 + 9 + 8 = 8
7 + 3 + 4 = 4
5 + 6 + 2 = 3

Puzzle #7

7 + 8 + 3 = 8
4 + 9 + 1 = 4
2 + 5 + 6 = 3
8 + 6 + 2 = 6
1 + 4 + 7 = 2
9 + 3 + 5 = 7
3 + 7 + 9 = 9
6 + 1 + 4 = 1
5 + 2 + 8 = 5

Puzzle #8

9 + 1 + 5 =
3 + 6 + 2 =
7 + 8 + 4 =
1 + 7 + 8 =
4 + 2 + 6 =
5 + 3 + 9 =
2 + 9 + 7 =
6 + 5 + 3 =
8 + 4 + 1 =

Puzzle #9

1 + 2 + 5 = 8
8 + 9 + 6 = 3
7 + 3 + 4 = 4
6 + 8 + 7 = 1
2 + 4 + 9 = 5
5 + 1 + 3 = 9
3 + 6 + 8 = 7
4 + 7 + 1 = 2
9 + 5 + 2 = 6

Puzzle #10

8 + 4 + 9 = 1
7 + 3 + 5 = 5
2 + 6 + 1 = 9
3 + 2 + 8 = 3
5 + 7 + 6 = 8
9 + 1 + 4 = 4
4 + 5 + 3 = 2
1 + 9 + 7 = 7
6 + 8 + 2 = 6

Puzzle #11

7 + 3 + 5 = 5
6 + 9 + 8 = 3
4 + 2 + 1 = 7
5 + 8 + 9 = 2
2 + 4 + 3 = 9
1 + 6 + 7 = 4
9 + 5 + 2 = 6
3 + 1 + 4 = 8
8 + 7 + 6 = 1

Puzzle #12

4 + 1 + 2 = 7
6 + 3 + 7 = 6
5 + 8 + 9 = 2
1 + 9 + 3 = 3
7 + 5 + 6 = 8
2 + 4 + 8 = 4
3 + 7 + 1 = 1
9 + 6 + 4 = 9
8 + 2 + 5 = 5

Puzzle #13

_ + 3 + 9 = 3
_ + 5 + 4 = 7
_ + 6 + 7 = 5
_ + 9 + 8 = 2
_ + 1 + 6 = 4
_ + 4 + 2 = 9
_ + 8 + 1 = 8
_ + 7 + 5 = 6
_ + 2 + 3 = 1

Puzzle #14

1 + 9 + 6 = 6
2 + 5 + 4 = 1
7 + 3 + 8 = 8
4 + 7 + 1 = 2
3 + 6 + 5 = 4
9 + 8 + 2 = 9
6 + 2 + 9 = 7
5 + 1 + 7 = 3
8 + 4 + 3 = 5

Puzzle #15

3 + 8 + 1 = 2
6 + 2 + 9 = 7
7 + 4 + 5 = 6
1 + 6 + 7 = 4
9 + 5 + 4 = 8
8 + 3 + 2 = 3
4 + 9 + 8 = 1
5 + 1 + 3 = 9
2 + 7 + 6 = 5

Puzzle #16

8 + 4 + 6 = 8
9 + 2 + 5 = 6
3 + 1 + 7 = 1
5 + 8 + 9 = 2
7 + 6 + 1 = 4
2 + 3 + 4 = 9
4 + 5 + 8 = 7
6 + 7 + 2 = 5
1 + 9 + 3 = 3

Puzzle #17

7 + 1 + 9 = 7
4 + 6 + 5 = 5
2 + 8 + 3 = 3
9 + 3 + 4 = 6
1 + 2 + 8 = 1
5 + 7 + 6 = 8
8 + 4 + 2 = 4
3 + 9 + 7 = 9
6 + 5 + 1 = 2

Puzzle #18

5 + 8 + 1 = 4
3 + 4 + 2 = 9
6 + 9 + 7 = 2
1 + 7 + 5 = 3
9 + 2 + 6 = 7
4 + 3 + 8 = 5
7 + 1 + 3 = 1
2 + 5 + 9 = 6
8 + 6 + 4 = 8

Puzzle #19

6 + 4 + 3 = 3
1 + 5 + 9 = 5
7 + 2 + 8 = 7
4 + 3 + 7 = 4
9 + 8 + 5 = 2
2 + 6 + 1 = 9
5 + 9 + 2 = 6
8 + 7 + 6 = 1
3 + 1 + 4 = 8

Puzzle #20

5 + 6 + 7 = 8
9 + 1 + 3 = 3
2 + 4 + 8 = 4
7 + 5 + 4 = 6
1 + 9 + 2 = 2
8 + 3 + 6 = 7
3 + 7 + 1 = 1
6 + 8 + 5 = 9
4 + 2 + 9 = 5

Puzzle #21

9 + 1 + 7 = 7
6 + 8 + 2 = 6
5 + 4 + 3 = 2
7 + 3 + 4 = 4
8 + 6 + 9 = 3
2 + 5 + 1 = 8
3 + 7 + 5 = 5
4 + 9 + 8 = 1
1 + 2 + 6 = 9

Puzzle #22

4 + 1 + 6 = 1
8 + 3 + 5 = 6
2 + 9 + 7 = 8
3 + 6 + 8 = 7
5 + 7 + 1 = 3
9 + 2 + 4 = 5
6 + 4 + 9 = 9
1 + 8 + 3 = 2
7 + 5 + 2 = 4

Puzzle #23

8 + 4 + 5 = 7
3 + 1 + 9 = 3
2 + 6 + 7 = 5
9 + 5 + 4 = 8
6 + 7 + 8 = 1
1 + 2 + 3 = 6
5 + 8 + 6 = 9
4 + 9 + 1 = 4
7 + 3 + 2 = 2

Puzzle #24

7 + 9 + 8 = 4
2 + 6 + 5 = 3
4 + 3 + 1 = 8
8 + 1 + 7 = 6
6 + 2 + 9 = 7
3 + 5 + 4 = 2
1 + 7 + 3 = 1
9 + 8 + 2 = 9
5 + 4 + 6 = 5

Puzzle #25

$9 + 3 + 5 = 7$
$8 + 7 + 1 = 6$
$2 + 4 + 6 = 2$
$4 + 6 + 9 = 9$
$5 + 8 + 2 = 5$
$3 + 1 + 7 = 1$
$6 + 9 + 3 = 8$
$7 + 2 + 4 = 3$
$1 + 5 + 8 = 4$

Puzzle #26

$6 + 3 + 7 = 6$
$4 + 9 + 8 = 1$
$5 + 2 + 1 = 8$
$2 + 4 + 3 = 9$
$8 + 5 + 9 = 2$
$1 + 7 + 6 = 4$
$7 + 8 + 2 = 7$
$9 + 1 + 5 = 5$
$3 + 6 + 4 = 3$

Puzzle #27

$6 + 1 + 4 = 1$
$8 + 7 + 3 = 8$
$2 + 9 + 5 = 6$
$5 + 6 + 8 = 9$
$3 + 2 + 7 = 2$
$9 + 4 + 1 = 4$
$4 + 5 + 6 = 5$
$7 + 8 + 2 = 7$
$1 + 3 + 9 = 3$

Puzzle #28

$4 + 6 + 1 =$
$3 + 7 + 5 =$
$9 + 8 + 2 =$
$8 + 2 + 4 =$
$6 + 5 + 7 =$
$1 + 3 + 9 =$
$2 + 9 + 6 =$
$5 + 4 + 3 =$
$7 + 1 + 8 =$

Puzzle #29

$6 + 3 + 7 = 6$
$2 + 4 + 5 = 1$
$1 + 9 + 8 = 8$
$7 + 6 + 1 = 4$
$8 + 2 + 9 = 9$
$3 + 5 + 4 = 2$
$5 + 7 + 3 = 5$
$9 + 8 + 6 = 3$
$4 + 1 + 2 = 7$

Puzzle #30

$1 + 4 + 6 = 1$
$8 + 5 + 2 = 5$
$3 + 7 + 9 = 9$
$7 + 6 + 5 = 8$
$2 + 3 + 8 = 3$
$9 + 1 + 4 = 4$
$4 + 2 + 1 = 7$
$6 + 9 + 7 = 2$
$5 + 8 + 3 = 6$

Puzzle #31

$2 + 7 + 9 = 8$
$1 + 8 + 4 = 3$
$5 + 3 + 6 = 4$
$8 + 6 + 3 = 7$
$9 + 2 + 5 = 6$
$7 + 4 + 1 = 2$
$6 + 1 + 2 = 9$
$3 + 5 + 7 = 5$
$4 + 9 + 8 = 1$

Puzzle #32

$8 + 9 + 7 = 4$
$5 + 3 + 4 = 2$
$6 + 2 + 1 = 9$
$7 + 1 + 3 = 1$
$2 + 5 + 9 = 6$
$4 + 6 + 8 = 8$
$9 + 4 + 2 = 5$
$3 + 8 + 6 = 7$
$1 + 7 + 5 = 3$

Puzzle #33

$3 + 4 + 2 = 9$
$8 + 9 + 5 = 2$
$6 + 1 + 7 = 4$
$9 + 8 + 4 = 1$
$2 + 3 + 1 = 6$
$5 + 7 + 6 = 8$
$1 + 5 + 9 = 5$
$7 + 2 + 8 = 7$
$4 + 6 + 3 = 3$

Puzzle #34

$5 + 4 + 3 = 2$
$6 + 1 + 2 = 9$
$7 + 8 + 9 = 4$
$2 + 9 + 4 = 5$
$1 + 5 + 7 = 3$
$3 + 6 + 8 = 7$
$4 + 3 + 1 = 8$
$8 + 7 + 6 = 1$
$9 + 2 + 5 = 6$

Puzzle #35

$5 + 8 + 6 = 9$
$9 + 1 + 4 = 4$
$2 + 3 + 7 = 2$
$3 + 2 + 1 = 6$
$4 + 5 + 9 = 8$
$7 + 6 + 8 = 1$
$1 + 9 + 3 = 3$
$6 + 4 + 5 = 5$
$8 + 7 + 2 = 7$

Puzzle #36

$5 + 1 + 9 = 5$
$7 + 4 + 6 = 7$
$3 + 8 + 2 = 3$
$9 + 7 + 3 = 9$
$2 + 6 + 4 = 2$
$8 + 5 + 1 = 4$
$4 + 2 + 5 = 1$
$6 + 3 + 7 = 6$
$1 + 9 + 8 = 8$

Puzzle #37

_ + 3 + 7 = 9
_ + 2 + 4 = 2
_ + 1 + 8 = 4
_ + 6 + 2 = 1
_ + 8 + 9 = 8
_ + 7 + 5 = 6
_ + 9 + 6 = 3
_ + 5 + 3 = 5
_ + 4 + 1 = 7

Puzzle #38

5 + 7 + 2 = 4
1 + 4 + 3 = 8
6 + 9 + 8 = 3
7 + 5 + 4 = 6
8 + 3 + 1 = 2
9 + 2 + 6 = 7
2 + 8 + 9 = 9
4 + 6 + 5 = 5
3 + 1 + 7 = 1

Puzzle #39

6 + 1 + 5 = 2
7 + 4 + 8 = 9
9 + 3 + 2 = 4
5 + 9 + 1 = 5
8 + 2 + 3 = 3
4 + 7 + 6 = 7
3 + 8 + 7 = 8
2 + 5 + 9 = 6
1 + 6 + 4 = 1

Puzzle #40

9 + 6 + 1 = 6
2 + 4 + 5 = 1
3 + 7 + 8 = 8
5 + 3 + 7 = 5
6 + 9 + 2 = 7
8 + 1 + 4 = 3
7 + 8 + 9 = 4
4 + 2 + 6 = 2
1 + 5 + 3 = 9

Puzzle #41

_ + 6 + 9 = 9
_ + 1 + 7 = 1
_ + 5 + 8 = 5
_ + 9 + 2 = 8
_ + 8 + 5 = 4
_ + 4 + 3 = 3
_ + 2 + 1 = 2
_ + 7 + 4 = 6
_ + 3 + 6 = 7

Puzzle #42

5 + 8 + 3 = 6
2 + 1 + 9 = 2
7 + 6 + 4 = 7
4 + 9 + 8 = 1
3 + 7 + 5 = 5
1 + 2 + 6 = 9
9 + 3 + 1 = 3
8 + 4 + 2 = 4
6 + 5 + 7 = 8

Puzzle #43

8 + 5 + 3 = 6
1 + 9 + 7 = 7
6 + 4 + 2 = 2
3 + 7 + 8 = 8
9 + 1 + 4 = 4
5 + 2 + 6 = 3
7 + 3 + 5 = 5
2 + 8 + 9 = 9
4 + 6 + 1 = 1

Puzzle #44

7 + 5 + 4 = 6
1 + 8 + 9 = 8
3 + 6 + 2 = 1
5 + 1 + 6 = 2
2 + 9 + 3 = 4
4 + 7 + 8 = 9
8 + 2 + 5 = 5
6 + 4 + 7 = 7
9 + 3 + 1 = 3

Puzzle #45

9 + 7 + 1 = 7
4 + 6 + 5 = 5
3 + 2 + 8 = 3
6 + 5 + 3 = 4
8 + 4 + 7 = 9
2 + 1 + 9 = 2
1 + 3 + 4 = 8
7 + 8 + 6 = 1
5 + 9 + 2 = 6

Puzzle #46

6 + 1 + 5 = 2
4 + 3 + 2 = 9
8 + 9 + 7 = 4
3 + 7 + 6 = 6
9 + 8 + 4 = 1
5 + 2 + 1 = 8
1 + 4 + 8 = 3
2 + 6 + 9 = 7
7 + 5 + 3 = 5

Puzzle #47

8 + 2 + 1 = 1
6 + 4 + 5 = 5
7 + 9 + 3 = 9
3 + 1 + 2 = 6
4 + 5 + 8 = 7
9 + 6 + 7 = 2
5 + 3 + 6 = 4
1 + 8 + 4 = 3
2 + 7 + 9 = 8

Puzzle #48

7 + 8 + 1 = 6
3 + 2 + 6 = 1
5 + 9 + 4 = 8
6 + 4 + 3 = 3
2 + 5 + 8 = 5
9 + 1 + 7 = 7
1 + 3 + 5 = 9
4 + 6 + 2 = 2
8 + 7 + 9 = 4

Puzzle #49

4 + 5 + 6 = 5
3 + 1 + 7 = 1
2 + 8 + 9 = 9
5 + 4 + 3 = 2
8 + 7 + 2 = 7
6 + 9 + 1 = 6
1 + 2 + 5 = 8
9 + 6 + 8 = 3
7 + 3 + 4 = 4

Puzzle #50

2 + 6 + 9 = 7
4 + 8 + 1 = 3
7 + 3 + 5 = 5
6 + 5 + 8 = 9
9 + 1 + 2 = 2
3 + 7 + 4 = 4
8 + 2 + 6 = 6
1 + 4 + 3 = 8
5 + 9 + 7 = 1

Puzzle #51

6 + 7 + 5 = 8
2 + 9 + 3 = 4
8 + 4 + 1 = 3
4 + 8 + 9 = 1
3 + 5 + 7 = 5
1 + 2 + 6 = 9
9 + 6 + 2 = 7
5 + 3 + 8 = 6
7 + 1 + 4 = 2

Puzzle #52

1 + 3 + 8 =
4 + 6 + 9 =
2 + 7 + 5 =
3 + 9 + 6 =
7 + 5 + 4 =
8 + 2 + 1 =
5 + 1 + 7 = 3
6 + 8 + 3 =
9 + 4 + 2 = 5

Puzzle #53

7 + 1 + 9 = 7
4 + 5 + 3 = 2
2 + 8 + 6 = 6
6 + 4 + 5 = 5
3 + 9 + 7 = 9
1 + 2 + 8 = 1
8 + 6 + 4 = 8
5 + 7 + 1 = 3
9 + 3 + 2 = 4

Puzzle #54

2 + 1 + 6 = 9
5 + 3 + 7 = 5
8 + 4 + 9 = 1
7 + 8 + 3 = 8
1 + 9 + 4 = 4
6 + 2 + 5 = 3
4 + 7 + 1 = 2
9 + 5 + 2 = 6
3 + 6 + 8 = 7

Puzzle #55

2 + 5 + 1 = 8
7 + 6 + 3 = 6
9 + 8 + 4 = 1
6 + 4 + 7 = 7
3 + 1 + 9 = 3
5 + 2 + 8 = 5
1 + 7 + 6 = 4
8 + 9 + 5 = 2
4 + 3 + 2 = 9

Puzzle #56

5 + 8 + 9 = 2
7 + 6 + 4 = 7
3 + 2 + 1 = 6
6 + 7 + 8 = 1
1 + 5 + 3 = 9
9 + 4 + 2 = 5
8 + 9 + 7 = 4
2 + 1 + 5 = 8
4 + 3 + 6 = 3

Puzzle #57

5 + 6 + 7 = 8
4 + 1 + 9 = 4
3 + 2 + 8 = 3
2 + 4 + 6 = 2
7 + 8 + 1 = 6
9 + 3 + 5 = 7
8 + 5 + 2 = 5
1 + 7 + 3 = 1
6 + 9 + 4 = 9

Puzzle #58

8 + 2 + 4 = 4
7 + 9 + 3 = 9
6 + 1 + 5 = 2
2 + 6 + 9 = 7
3 + 5 + 7 = 5
4 + 8 + 1 = 3
5 + 4 + 2 = 1
1 + 7 + 8 = 6
9 + 3 + 6 = 8

Puzzle #59

8 + 7 + 6 = 1
1 + 9 + 5 = 5
3 + 2 + 4 = 9
2 + 5 + 7 = 4
6 + 4 + 8 = 8
9 + 3 + 1 = 3
4 + 6 + 2 = 2
5 + 8 + 3 = 6
7 + 1 + 9 = 7

Puzzle #60

4 + 7 + 2 = 3
6 + 8 + 1 = 5
5 + 9 + 3 = 7
2 + 4 + 5 = 1
7 + 1 + 8 = 6
3 + 6 + 9 = 8
8 + 2 + 4 = 4
1 + 5 + 6 = 2
9 + 3 + 7 = 5

Puzzle #61

$+ 1 + 7 = 4$
$+ 3 + 8 = 3$
$+ 4 + 5 = 8$
$+ 9 + 3 = 7$
$+ 8 + 1 = 6$
$+ 6 + 2 = 2$
$+ 5 + 9 = 5$
$+ 7 + 4 = 9$
$+ 2 + 6 = 1$

Puzzle #62

$4 + 3 + 6 = 3$
$1 + 9 + 5 = 5$
$8 + 2 + 7 = 7$
$3 + 7 + 8 = 8$
$2 + 5 + 4 = 1$
$9 + 6 + 1 = 6$
$6 + 1 + 2 = 9$
$7 + 8 + 9 = 4$
$5 + 4 + 3 = 2$

Puzzle #63

$7 + 6 + 5 = 8$
$1 + 3 + 9 = 3$
$4 + 2 + 8 = 4$
$3 + 4 + 2 = 9$
$8 + 7 + 6 = 1$
$9 + 5 + 1 = 5$
$6 + 9 + 7 = 2$
$5 + 8 + 4 = 7$
$2 + 1 + 3 = 6$

Puzzle #64

$7 + 1 + 4 = 2$
$6 + 5 + 8 = 9$
$3 + 9 + 2 = 4$
$5 + 7 + 3 = 5$
$2 + 4 + 1 = 7$
$9 + 8 + 6 = 3$
$1 + 2 + 5 = 8$
$8 + 6 + 7 = 1$
$4 + 3 + 9 = 6$

Puzzle #65

$+ 9 + 7 = 1$
$+ 6 + 1 = 9$
$+ 3 + 8 = 5$
$+ 2 + 4 = 7$
$+ 7 + 9 = 2$
$+ 8 + 5 = 6$
$+ 5 + 6 = 8$
$+ 4 + 2 = 4$
$+ 1 + 3 = 3$

Puzzle #66

$6 + 7 + 8 = 1$
$1 + 5 + 2 = 8$
$9 + 3 + 4 = 6$
$5 + 8 + 6 = 9$
$3 + 4 + 7 = 4$
$2 + 9 + 1 = 2$
$8 + 2 + 3 = 3$
$7 + 1 + 9 = 7$
$4 + 6 + 5 = 5$

Puzzle #67

$7 + 4 + 1 = 2$
$6 + 2 + 8 = 6$
$5 + 9 + 3 = 7$
$3 + 6 + 9 = 8$
$2 + 7 + 4 = 3$
$1 + 8 + 5 = 4$
$4 + 5 + 6 = 5$
$9 + 3 + 7 = 9$
$8 + 1 + 2 = 1$

Puzzle #68

$1 + 5 + 9 = 5$
$4 + 6 + 7 = 7$
$8 + 3 + 2 = 3$
$6 + 7 + 5 = 8$
$2 + 8 + 1 = 1$
$9 + 4 + 3 = 6$
$5 + 9 + 8 = 2$
$3 + 2 + 4 = 9$
$7 + 1 + 6 = 4$

Puzzle #69

$7 + 5 + 4 = 6$
$9 + 2 + 6 = 7$
$1 + 3 + 8 = 2$
$2 + 4 + 3 = 9$
$5 + 9 + 7 = 1$
$8 + 6 + 1 = 5$
$4 + 8 + 2 = 4$
$3 + 1 + 9 = 3$
$6 + 7 + 5 = 8$

Puzzle #70

$7 + 2 + 6 = 5$
$9 + 3 + 1 = 3$
$5 + 4 + 8 = 7$
$4 + 5 + 7 = 6$
$3 + 6 + 2 = 1$
$8 + 1 + 9 = 8$
$2 + 9 + 3 = 4$
$1 + 7 + 4 = 2$
$6 + 8 + 5 = 9$

Puzzle #71

$3 + 8 + 1 = 2$
$7 + 4 + 5 = 6$
$2 + 9 + 6 = 7$
$5 + 1 + 7 = 3$
$9 + 6 + 3 = 8$
$4 + 2 + 8 = 4$
$6 + 3 + 2 = 1$
$1 + 5 + 9 = 5$
$8 + 7 + 4 = 9$

Puzzle #72

$3 + 4 + 2 = 9$
$5 + 8 + 9 = 2$
$6 + 7 + 1 = 4$
$9 + 3 + 4 = 6$
$2 + 1 + 5 = 8$
$8 + 6 + 7 = 1$
$4 + 5 + 8 = 7$
$1 + 9 + 3 = 3$
$7 + 2 + 6 = 5$

Puzzle #73
6 + 9 + 3 = 8
8 + 5 + 1 = 4
7 + 2 + 4 = 3
9 + 8 + 5 = 2
4 + 6 + 7 = 7
1 + 3 + 2 = 6
2 + 1 + 8 = 1
3 + 7 + 9 = 9
5 + 4 + 6 = 5

Puzzle #74
2 + 9 + 6 = 7
7 + 5 + 3 = 5
4 + 1 + 8 = 3
9 + 8 + 7 = 4
6 + 2 + 4 = 2
1 + 3 + 5 = 9
3 + 4 + 1 = 8
5 + 7 + 9 = 1
8 + 6 + 2 = 6

Puzzle #75
4 + 8 + 9 = 1
1 + 2 + 5 = 8
3 + 7 + 6 = 6
2 + 4 + 8 = 4
5 + 3 + 1 = 9
6 + 9 + 7 = 2
7 + 5 + 3 = 5
9 + 6 + 2 = 7
8 + 1 + 4 = 3

Puzzle #76
7 + 9 + 1 =
2 + 6 + 8 =
4 + 3 + 5 =
6 + 1 + 7 =
8 + 2 + 3 =
9 + 5 + 4 =
3 + 7 + 9 =
1 + 8 + 6 =
5 + 4 + 2 =

Puzzle #77
3 + 2 + 9 = 4
4 + 8 + 6 = 8
5 + 1 + 7 = 3
6 + 7 + 2 = 5
1 + 5 + 3 = 9
8 + 9 + 4 = 1
7 + 4 + 1 = 2
9 + 3 + 5 = 7
2 + 6 + 8 = 6

Puzzle #78
7 + 2 + 3 = 2
4 + 1 + 9 = 4
8 + 6 + 5 = 9
5 + 4 + 6 = 5
9 + 3 + 1 = 3
2 + 8 + 7 = 7
6 + 7 + 8 = 1
3 + 9 + 4 = 6
1 + 5 + 2 = 8

Puzzle #79
6 + 5 + 3 = 4
7 + 2 + 9 = 8
8 + 4 + 1 = 3
2 + 9 + 8 = 9
1 + 6 + 4 = 1
5 + 3 + 7 = 5
3 + 7 + 6 = 6
4 + 8 + 5 = 7
9 + 1 + 2 = 2

Puzzle #80
2 + 5 + 6 = 3
3 + 8 + 4 = 5
7 + 1 + 9 = 7
9 + 4 + 3 = 6
6 + 7 + 8 = 1
5 + 2 + 1 = 8
8 + 6 + 5 = 9
4 + 3 + 7 = 4
1 + 9 + 2 = 2

Puzzle #81
2 + 6 + 4 = 2
5 + 1 + 3 = 9
8 + 9 + 7 = 4
6 + 2 + 8 = 6
7 + 3 + 1 = 1
9 + 4 + 5 = 8
3 + 8 + 2 = 3
4 + 5 + 6 = 5
1 + 7 + 9 = 7

Puzzle #82
6 + 3 + 4 = 3
1 + 5 + 8 = 4
7 + 2 + 9 = 8
3 + 8 + 5 = 6
9 + 7 + 1 = 7
2 + 4 + 6 = 2
8 + 6 + 7 = 1
4 + 9 + 2 = 5
5 + 1 + 3 = 9

Puzzle #83
7 + 3 + 5 = 5
6 + 8 + 9 = 3
4 + 2 + 1 = 7
2 + 4 + 3 = 9
8 + 9 + 7 = 4
1 + 5 + 6 = 2
3 + 6 + 2 = 1
9 + 1 + 8 = 8
5 + 7 + 4 = 6

Puzzle #84
2 + 6 + 4 = 2
7 + 9 + 1 = 7
5 + 8 + 3 = 6
1 + 3 + 9 = 3
6 + 7 + 5 = 8
4 + 2 + 8 = 4
3 + 4 + 2 = 9
8 + 1 + 6 = 5
9 + 5 + 7 = 5

Puzzle #85

	+ 5 + 6 =		4
	+ 1 + 4 =		2
	+ 9 + 2 =		9
	+ 3 + 1 =		6
	+ 6 + 7 =		8
	+ 4 + 8 =		1
	+ 2 + 5 =		3
	+ 7 + 9 =		7
	+ 8 + 3 =		5

Puzzle #86

2 + 7 + 8 =	7
6 + 9 + 1 =	6
3 + 4 + 5 =	2
1 + 5 + 3 =	9
7 + 2 + 6 =	5
9 + 8 + 4 =	1
4 + 1 + 9 =	4
8 + 3 + 7 =	8
5 + 6 + 2 =	3

Puzzle #87

1 + 6 + 8 =	5
5 + 4 + 2 =	1
7 + 3 + 9 =	9
4 + 2 + 7 =	3
3 + 5 + 6 =	4
9 + 8 + 1 =	8
2 + 9 + 5 =	6
6 + 7 + 4 =	7
8 + 1 + 3 =	2

Puzzle #88

7 + 2 + 9 =	8
8 + 3 + 5 =	6
6 + 1 + 4 =	1
3 + 4 + 7 =	4
9 + 5 + 8 =	2
2 + 6 + 1 =	9
4 + 7 + 2 =	3
1 + 8 + 6 =	5
5 + 9 + 3 =	7

Puzzle #89

	+ 3 + 7 =		6
	+ 9 + 8 =		1
	+ 2 + 1 =		8
	+ 4 + 3 =		9
	+ 5 + 9 =		2
	+ 7 + 6 =		4
	+ 8 + 2 =		7
9 + 1 + 5 =		5
3 + 6 + 4 =		3

Puzzle #90

1 + 4 + 6 =	1
2 + 5 + 9 =	6
3 + 7 + 8 =	8
4 + 2 + 3 =	9
5 + 8 + 1 =	4
6 + 9 + 7 =	2
7 + 6 + 2 =	5
8 + 1 + 4 =	3
9 + 3 + 5 =	7

Islands #1

	+ 2 + 7 =	9
4 + 3 + 6 =		3
8 + 9 + 5 =		2
9 + 5 +	=	4
6 + 7 + 2 =		5
3 + 4 + 1 =		8
7 + 6 + 3 =		6
2 +	+ 9 =	1
5 + 8 + 4 =		7

Islands #2

1 + 7 + 8 =	6
4 + 6 + 3 =	3
2 + 9 +	=	1
	+ 8 + 1 =	9
9 + 4 + 2 =	5
6 + 5 + 7 =	8
8 +	+ 4 =	2
7 + 1 + 6 =	4
5 + 3 + 9 =	7

Islands #3

6 + 8 + 4 =	8
3 +	+ 9 =	2
7 + 1 + 5 =	3
	+ 7 + 2 =	9
8 + 6 + 1 =	5
9 + 4 + 3 =	6
2 + 5 + 7 =	4
1 +	+ 6 =	7
4 + 9 + 8 =	1

Islands #4

6 + 8 + 5 =	9
1 + 9 + 2 =	2
4 +	+ 7 =	1
3 + 5 + 9 =	7
2 + 4 + 8 =	4
7 + 1 +	=	8
9 + 7 +	=	6
8 + 2 + 3 =	3
5 + 6 + 4 =	5

No Fives #1

9 + 4 + 8 =	1
2 + 3 + 1 =	6
0 + 6 + 7 =	3
6 + 1 + 3 =	0
7 + 2 + 9 =	8
4 + 8 + 0 =	2
3 + 0 + 4 =	7
1 + 7 + 6 =	4
8 + 9 + 2 =	9

No Fives #2

9 + 8 + 3 =	0
0 + 6 + 2 =	8
7 + 4 + 1 =	2
3 + 0 + 8 =	1
4 + 2 + 7 =	3
1 + 9 + 6 =	6
2 + 3 + 9 =	4
6 + 1 + 0 =	7
8 + 7 + 4 =	9

No Fives #3

1 + 7 + 3 =		1
0 + 4 + 2 =		6
9 + 6 + 8 =		3
2 + 9 + 7 =		8
4 + 8 + 0 =		2
6 + 3 + 1 =		0
8 + 2 + 4 =		4
7 + 1 + 9 =		7
3 + 0 + 6 =		9

No Fives #4

1 + 4 + 8 =		3
0 + 3 + 6 =		9
2 + 9 + 7 =		8
7 + 0 + 9 =		6
6 + 1 + 3 =		0
8 + 2 + 4 =		4
9 + 7 + 1 =		7
4 + 8 + 0 =		2
3 + 6 + 2 =		1

Hide & Seek #1

6 + 2 + 3 =		1
7 + 4 + 8 =		9
9 + 5 + 1 =		5
2 + 9 + 6 =		7
1 + 8 + 7 =		6
5 + 3 + 4 =		2
8 + 1 + 5 =		4
3 + 6 + 9 =		8
4 + 7 + 2 =		3

Hide & Seek #2

6 + 5 + 7 =	
3 + 2 + 8 =	
9 + 4 + 1 =	
1 + 7 + 3 =	
4 + 6 + 9 =	
5 + 8 + 2 =	
7 + 1 + 4 =	
8 + 3 + 5 =	
2 + 9 + 6 =	

Hide & Seek #3

2 + 4 + 1 =		7
6 + 9 + 8 =		3
3 + 7 + 5 =		5
8 + 1 + 2 =		1
9 + 3 + 4 =		6
7 + 5 + 6 =		8
4 + 6 + 9 =		9
5 + 2 + 7 =		4
1 + 8 + 3 =		2

Hide & Seek #4

6 + 1 + 2 =		9
7 + 5 + 9 =		1
4 + 3 + 8 =		5
2 + 9 + 7 =		8
3 + 6 + 5 =		4
1 + 8 + 4 =		3
8 + 7 + 1 =		6
5 + 4 + 3 =		2
9 + 2 + 6 =		7

	1	9	5	7	6	2	4	3	8	
9	1	3	5	4	2	6	9	8	7	4
1	8	9	4	5	3	7	1	2	6	9
5	2	7	6	8	1	9	4	3	5	2
6	9	6	1				5	7	1	3
7	5	4	8				2	4	9	5
2	7	2	3				3	6	8	7
4	4	8	2	5	7	1	6	9	3	8
8	6	5	7	3	4	9	8	1	2	1
3	3	1	9	8	6	2	7	5	4	6
	3	4	8	6	7	2	1	5	9	

Krazy Kansuko #2

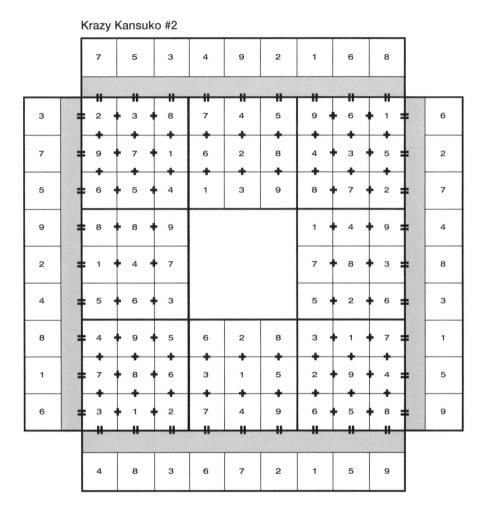

Bonus Puzzles!

Enjoy a sneak peek at the next new puzzle from Jonathan Meck!

Instructions: Add operation signs between the numbers on the outside of the square: plus signs (+), minus signs (-), multiplication signs (x), or division signs (/). **Follow order of operations** for each side of the square, making sure the last digit equals the number in the center of the square. For instance, if 2 was in the center of the square, each side would have to equate to something with a 2 in the singles column (Ex: -2, 12, 52, -32). The solution on each side of the square can be positive or negative but will be less than 100. You only need to worry about whole numbers while multiplying and dividing; you'll never need to use fractions or decimals.

There is only one solution for each of these puzzles.

EXAMPLE:

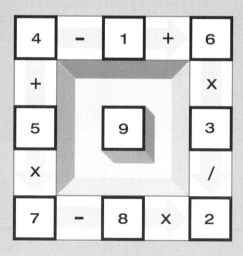

$$4 - 1 + 6 = 9$$

$$4 + 5 \times 7 = 39$$

$$6 \times 3 / 2 = 9$$

$$7 - 8 \times 2 = -9$$

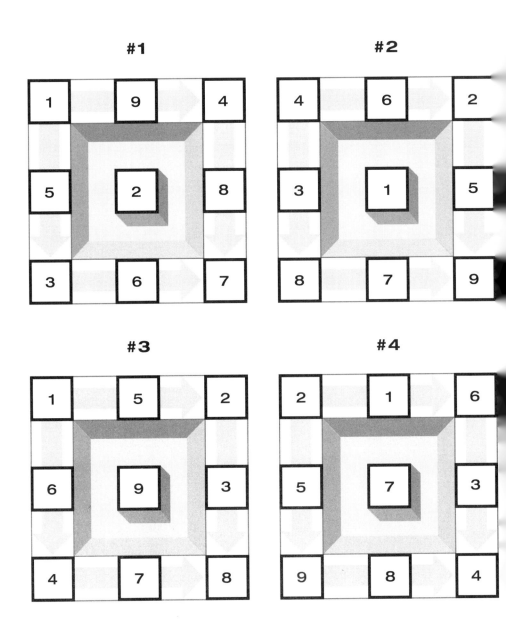

#1

1	9	4
5	2	8
3	6	7

#2

4	6	2
3	1	5
8	7	9

#3

1	5	2
6	9	3
4	7	8

#4

2	1	6
5	7	3
9	8	4

Solutions on page 144

#5

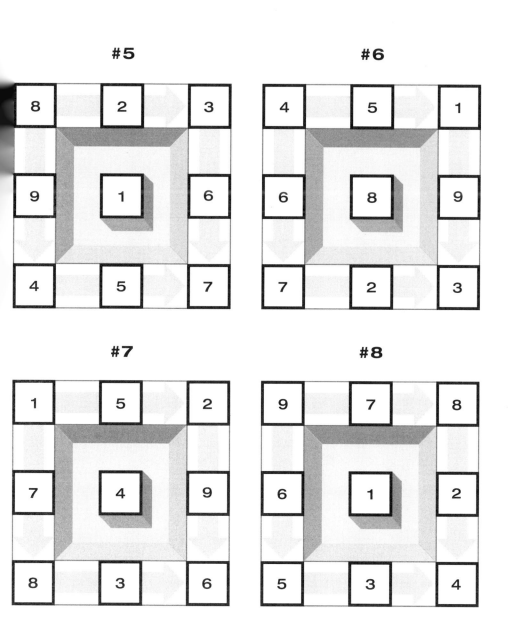

8	2	3
9	1	6
4	5	7

#6

4	5	1
6	8	9
7	2	3

#7

1	5	2
7	4	9
8	3	6

#8

9	7	8
6	1	2
5	3	4

Solutions on page 144

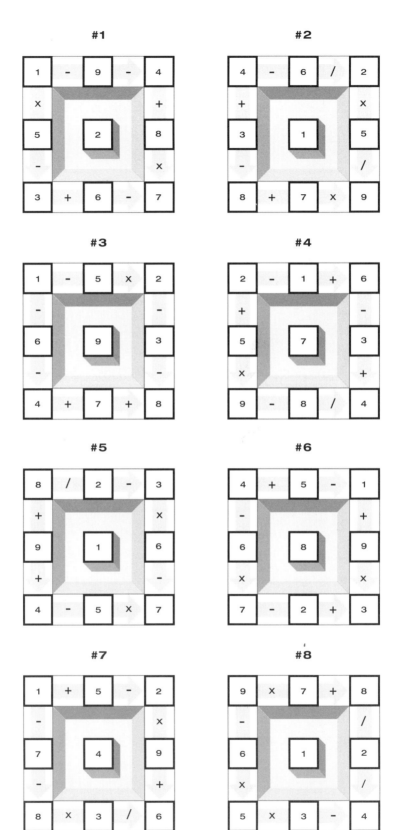